SEA
SNAKES

Unique sea creatures

REUBEN J. THOMPSON

Table of Contents

CHAPTER ONE

SEA SNAKES

Sea snakes are firmly identified with Cobras. they're sea-going rather than land abiding snakes. Genuine sea winds just sleep in water. Sea Snakes have adjusted daily existence in water and have little leveled heads that limits water opposition once they swim. the ocean Snakes body is packed as a variation for swimming and therefore the snakes are so altogether amphibian that they're either cumbersome or moderate when brought aground. Sea snake, any of in more than 60 sorts

of exceptionally venomous marine snakes of the cobra family (Elapidae). There are two autonomously developed gatherings: the real sea snakes (subfamily Hydrophiinae), which are identified with Australian earthbound elapids, and therefore the sea kraits (subfamily Laticaudinae), which are identified with the Asian cobras. In spite of the very fact that their toxin is that the most intense, all things considered, human fatalities are uncommon in light of the very fact that sea snakes aren't forceful, their toxin yield is small , and their teeth are exceptionally shy Of the 55 sorts of genuine sea snakes, most grown-ups are 1–1.5 meters (3.3–5 feet) long , however a couple of people may achieve 2.7 meters (8.9 feet). they're limited to waterfront spaces of the Indian and western Pacific seas, with the exception of the cowardly snake (Pelamis platurus), found in untamed sea from Africa toward the east across the Pacific toward the west shoreline of America . Any remaining species live for the foremost part in waters under 30 meters (around 100 feet) profound, as they ought to plunge to the ocean floor to urge their food among coral reefs, among mangroves, or on the ocean base. a couple of animal categories incline toward hard bottoms (corals), while others favor delicate bottoms (mud or sand) during which to chase their prey. Most ocean snakes plenty of different sizes and shapes, including eels. Two crude gatherings (genera Aipysurus and Emydocephalus) eat just fish eggs; Hydrophis has some expertise in tunneling eels. In transformation to marine life, genuine ocean snakes have a smoothed body with a brief oarlike tail, valvular nostrils on top of the nose, and lengthened lungs that expand the entire length of the body. Their scales are exceptionally little and usually not covering (compared), adjoining against one another like clearing stones. The paunch scales are decreased in size within the crude species, while within the further developed structures they're missing.

Accordingly, the high level species can't slither and are subsequently powerless ashore. When swimming, a fall is formed along a bit of the midsection, expanding surface region and helping drive, which happens by horizontal undulation. Sea snakes can stay lowered for a couple of hours, conceivably the maximum amount as a minimum of eight. this

excellent accomplishment is somewhat due to the way that they will inhale through their skin. In more than 90% of waste CO_2 and 33 percent of their oxygen prerequisite are often moved by means of cutaneous breath. additionally , an investigation of the blue-joined snake (or annulated ocean snake, Hydrophis cyanocinctus) discovered an exceptionally vascularized region between the nose and therefore the highest point of the top , which allows oxygen to be moved straightforwardly from the water to the snake's cerebrum. Ocean snakes conceive an offspring within the sea to a traditional of 2–9 youthful, however upwards of 34 could be conceived. The 54 species in subfamily Hydrophiinae have an area with 16 distinct general. The six sorts of ocean kraits (variety Laticauda) aren't as particular for amphibian life because the genuine ocean snakes. Albeit the tail is straightened, the body is barrel shaped, and therefore the nostrils are parallel. they need expanded midsection scales like those of earthly snakes and may creep and jump ashore. The run of the mill shading design comprises of exchanging groups of dark with dim, blue, or white rings. The yellow-lipped ocean krait (L. colubrina) may be a typical animal categories that has this

instance and features

a yellow nose. Ocean kraits are nighttime, taking care of principally on eels at profundities of under 15 meters (49 feet). they are going aground to get their eggs, ascending into limestone buckles and rock fissure, where they store 1–10 eggs. Grown-ups normal 1 meter long, yet some develop to quite 1.5 meters. The lifetime record in imprisonment is seven years. Hardly any zoos or people have had tons of progress saving ocean kraits for long, as they have enormous pools of warm salt water even as rocks and other dry zones on which to loll. they're genuinely versatile, nonetheless, and a couple of zoos have had moderate achievement utilizing new water with simply periodic showers in salt water. Water temperatures need to be around 80 degrees Fahrenheit, with land temperatures somewhere within the range of 80 and 90 degrees.

Lounging lights are going to be utilized by certain people. In nature the ocean kraits feed solely on eels of varied species, an eating routine difficult to coordinate in imprisonment. a couple of examples suits taking different sorts of stretched fish, yet taking care of are very often a big issue. Endeavors to vary ocean kraits to rodents for the foremost part fizzle. Despite the very fact that conceivably perilously venomous, this species has gained notoriety for being quiet, effectively took care of and creating almost no toxin. Nibbles are practically obscure, yet this doesn't mean the species need to be thought little of or addressed nonchalantly.

Numerous sorts of ocean snakes show markings and shading designs that are genuinely staggering while others are strong and dreary.

Sea snakes can accomplish a length of as long as 6.5 feet (2 m), yet most are just an outsized portion of this length or more limited. One gathering of ocean snakes, which is now then alluded to because the genuine ocean snakes, bear live youthful. These snakes come up short on the developed scales which will without much of a stretch be seen on most earthly snakes. the opposite gathering is understood as kraits (or ocean kraits). These creatures leave the water to mate and lay their eggs. Sea kraits have tie like body scales that are absent within the genuine ocean snakes. At the purpose when jumpers address one another in laymen's terms, some will utilize the expressions "sea kraits" and "kraits," yet the greater a part of us knot everything of the creatures into a solitary gathering of creatures we call ocean snakes. during this piece, except if I explicitly utilize the expressions "ocean kraits" or "kraits," it's right to expect that i'm gathering everything of the creatures once I utilize the expression "ocean snakes."

With toxin that's significantly more powerful than that of cobras, ocean snakes are among the foremost venomous creatures on earth. Luckily, notwithstanding, ocean snakes are once during a while forceful. In any case, little question about it, they're profoundly venomous, being provided with amazingly powerful neurotoxins.

It is uncommon for a jumper to urge nibbled, and truth be told it's undocumented for any jumpers or swimmers

that weren't taking   care   of
or that   did
not unintentionally tread
on ocean   snakes to
possess at any point been
chomped.   A   relentless
legend about ocean snakes
expresses   that they   can
not nibble alright in   light
of the   very   fact that   their
teeth are within the back of
mouths that are minuscule.
Not   thoroughly   evident.
Being 2.5-4.5 mm long, their
teeth   are actually more

limited than numerous earthly snakes, however their mouth and teeth are quite enough created to nibble a person's thigh, and that they regularly swallow fish that are quite twice the measurement of their own necks.

Most chomps and fatalities happen when anglers plan to eliminate an ocean snake snared in their nets. Most ocean snakes are somewhat powerless when ashore, however however they ought not be addressed . one among the more toxic species is that the Beaked snake . a traditional measured example can create 10-15 milligrams of toxin at anybody time, and 1.5 milligrams is perhaps getting to demonstrate deadly to people. Now and again ocean snakes show a sense of interest in jumpers, and it alright could also be a touch alarming once you see a snake that's undeniably more venomous than a cobra swimming right at you. For sure, it's ideal to understand that these creatures aren't forceful toward jumpers and swimmers who aren't getting or tread on them. Ocean snakes are extremely proficient swimmers, "S-ing" their way through the water in developments that appear just like

the development of
various earthbound   snakes.
Their   enlarged   and
straightened,   paddle-like
tail is   employed during
a paddle like style furnishing
them   with tons of   push.

CHAPTER TWO
CHARACTERISTICS

Sea Snakes are just reasonably enormous, infrequently surpassing 2 meters long, regularly with curiously little heads for his or her body size. Just sort 'Laticauda' (which incorporates the Black Banded Sea Krait) has the traditional expansive ventral sizes of snakes and it's regularly viewed because the most un-progressed of the ocean snakes. By and by, like cetaceans, their lungs actually expect them to surface infrequently to relax. Oxygen consumption through the skin has been exhibited in ocean snakes. Sea snakes like warm, tropical waters, notwithstanding, when the water gets excessively warm, they swim right down to cooler temperatures. Transmitters connected to cowardly ocean snakes show they will plunge to around 150 feet and may remain submerged for over three hours. Like seabirds and ocean turtles, ocean snakes have uncommon organs that gather additional salt from the blood. The snake's salt organs lie underneath their tongues. whenever an snake flicks its tongue, it's catapulting salt once more into the ocean .

Ocean snakes have particular straightened tails for swimming and have valves over their noses which are shut submerged. In contrast to eels, ocean snakes need gills or balances, rather having scales and investing tons of their energy submerged, they ought to surface consistently to relax.

CHAPTER THREE

HABITAT

Sea snakes are kept to the tropical seas, predominantly the Indian Ocean and therefore

the western Pacific . The cowardly ocean snake, (Pelamis platurus), reaches out toward the eastern Pacific. The olive ocean snake, (Aipysurus laevis), watches out for sleep in reefs.

CHAPTER FOUR
BEHAVIOR AND DIET

The cowardly ocean snake (Pelamis platurus) is pelagic (living in open seas or oceans as against waters neighboring area or inland waters) and is seen on events gliding in gigantic gatherings. Fish that surface to shield under slicks give food to the snakes. Periodically these cowardly sea snakes get appeared on sea shores after tempests and represent a peril to youngsters.

Sea snakes are forceful just during the mating season within the colder time of year, the ocean snake is extremely inquisitive and that they become entranced by prolonged items like high pressing factor hoses. The Sea snakes most loved food is fish. Ocean snakes follow fish (counting eels) and shellfish. Two or three species are had practical experience in eating fish eggs. Others are worked in eating certain fish species.

CHAPTER FIVE
REPRODUCTION

Aside from a solitary variety, all ocean snakes are ovoviviparous (improvement of eggs that stay inside the moms body up until they carry forth or are getting to incubate.). The youthful are conceived alive within the water where they experience as long as they will remember cycle. In certain species, the youthful are very enormous, here and

there up to half as long as
their mom. The one
exemption is that the class
'Laticauda', which are
oviparous (creatures that lay
eggs with next to zero other
undeveloped advancement
inside the mother). Its five
species all lay their eggs
ashore.

SEA SNAKE VENOM

Sea snakes might not be the
foremost venomous on the
earth , notwithstanding, their
toxin is more harmful than

that of Mojave diamondbacks and lord cobras. Ocean snakes toxin contains some of comparable synthetic substances found in cobra toxin, just more gathered in structure.

Made in United States
Troutdale, OR
01/30/2024

17316651R00022